# MEDIA WRITING HANDBOOK

## GUIDELINES FOR RADIO, TELEVISION & FILM SCRIPTS AND ACADEMIC PAPERS

Donald N. Wood

Department of Radio-Television-Film
College of Arts, Media, and Communication
California State University, Northridge

An academic manual designed for media majors to aid
in the preparation and writing of research papers and
scripts for all radio, television, and film courses

KENDALL/HUNT PUBLISHING COMPANY
4050 Westmark Drive    Dubuque, Iowa 52002

# Table of Contents

Preface . . . . . . . . . . . . . . . . . . . . . . . . . . . . . . . . . . . . v

1. The Write Attitude . . . . . . . . . . . . . . . . . . . . . . . . . . 1

2. On Understanding Directions . . . . . . . . . . . . . . . . . . . 1

3. Plagiarism and Honesty . . . . . . . . . . . . . . . . . . . . . . . 1

4. General Procedures . . . . . . . . . . . . . . . . . . . . . . . . . 2
   - Research Attitudes
   - Outlining
   - Idea and Word Processing
   - Drafting and Re-writing
   - Understanding Your Format
   - Eliminating Noise
   - Proofreading

5. Research Hints . . . . . . . . . . . . . . . . . . . . . . . . . . . . 3
   Research Sources
   - Electronic Sources
   - Note Cards
   Use of Footnotes or Endnotes

6. Format: the Academic Paper . . . . . . . . . . . . . . . . . . . . 4
   Covers and Title Pages
   Front Matter
   - Table of Contents
   - Outline
   - List of Figures or Illustrations
   End Matter
   - Endnotes
   - Appendixes
   - Bibliography
   Section Headings

7. Format: Scripts and Screenplays . . . . . . . . . . . . . . . . . 5
   The Cover Page
   Specific Format Requirements
   Supplemental Materials
   Sample Script Pages

8. Outlining . . . . . . . . . . . . . . . . . . . . . . . . . . . . . . . 5

9. Matters of Style . . . . . . . . . . . . . . . . . . . . . . . . . . . . . . . . . . . . . . . 6
    Style Manuals
    Formats for Notes and Bibliography
       • Internet Citations
    Other Stylistic Concerns

10. Writing Tips . . . . . . . . . . . . . . . . . . . . . . . . . . . . . . . . . . . . . . . . . 7

11. Appearance . . . . . . . . . . . . . . . . . . . . . . . . . . . . . . . . . . . . . . . . . 7
    Copy Quality
    Acceptable Fonts

Appendix A. Statement on Academic Honesty . . . . . . . . . . . . . . . . . . . . . 9

Appendix B. Miscellaneous Materials and Writing Guidelines . . . . . . . . . . . 11
    Outline Format: Guidelines
    Some Stylistic Concerns
    A Few Grammatical and Punctuation Considerations
    "29 Rules for Righting a Good Reserch Paper"

Appendix C. Sample Materials for an Academic Paper . . . . . . . . . . . . . . . 17
    Table of Contents
    Outline for Academic Paper
    Page of Academic Paper
    Bibliographic Formats

Appendix D. Sample Materials for Script Formats . . . . . . . . . . . . . . . . . . 23
    Film Format Template
    Situation Comedy Template
    Sample Script Format: Single-column Television
    Sample Script Format: Two-column Television
    Sample Script Format: Teleplay/Screenplay
    Sample Script Format: Instructional Film
    Sample Radio Format
    Script Excerpt
    Sample Premise

Bibliography . . . . . . . . . . . . . . . . . . . . . . . . . . . . . . . . . . . . . . . . . . 35

# Preface

This *Writing Handbook* has been created to assist students in media courses to prepare written materials for all class assignments. These "Guidelines for Radio, Television & Film Scripts and Academic Papers" are designed to help you in the writing of all research papers, reports, term papers, treatments, screenplays and other scripts throughout your entire academic career. These pages contain crucial format instructions, as well as helpful writing and stylistic hints.

Please read these guidelines carefully. They cover many fundamental matters of language usage and composition so that you can then get on with the creative job of writing your papers and scripts. This Handbook has been prepared to help all students deal with basic language and format questions. You must correctly handle the elements of format, design, outlining, grammar, sentence structure, punctuation, spelling, and other routine writing requirements before any instructor, producer, agent, publisher, or production staffer can evaluate your inventive and artistic talents. We want you to do the best job you can. We want you to succeed.

It is important for you to refer to this Handbook from your first media class through your final course before graduation. Faculty members may provide specific instructions not covered in this Handbook; but unless your instructor gives you some other precise directions, use this Handbook as your guide in all course work in your department.

Good luck. Good writing.

Judith Marlane, Chair
Radio-TV-Film Department
California State University, Northridge

# MEDIA WRITING HANDBOOK

This handbook is prepared for all media majors. These guidelines have been designed to be used for all written assignments—research reports, scripts and screenplays, term papers, and so forth. Writing is the foundation for all media projects—regardless of the production tools, the technologies, or the format of the final product. It all must start with the written word.

Students should follow these guidelines and procedures for assignments for *all* media courses. Except when faculty members require explicit formats or modifications for specific assignments, use this handbook as your bible.

## 1. THE WRITE ATTITUDE

College faculty are not put on earth just to harass media majors or to make life unnecessarily harsh. We are not sadists; we do not take pleasure in making you miserable. Believe it or not, we are here because we want to help you. We want to see you succeed in life—personally and professionally. And we know something about what it takes to succeed. So heed these words well.

First of all, take all writing assignments very seriously. The ability to write well—to clearly state your thesis, to formulate an argument, to organize material, to use the written language forcefully and clearly—is the best indication there is of an educated mind. This is true whether you are writing a dramatic screenplay or an academic research paper. Even if you manage to bluff your way through college without being able to write decently, you have fooled no one but yourself. You may have a degree, but you won't have the background, the confidence, the skills to declare yourself a professional in the field. *There is no shortcut; you must learn to write well if you want to succeed in any aspect of the media business.*

Second, the ability to write well is based on the ability to do good research. Research is not just the stuff of which dull academic papers are written. Research is the stuff from which human drama is created; it is the way that successful marketing campaigns are launched; the way new cultural perspectives are unearthed; the way that exciting discoveries are made; the way that personal growth is realized. If you cannot dig out information on your own, if you cannot explore uncharted academic and cultural waters, if you cannot analyze materials and evaluate what is handed to you, if you cannot look at a source and realize it is bogus, then you are destined forever to be someone else's cultural slave. You are not fit to be considered a free person and an independent thinker. You certainly are not

fit to be considered a media professional.

No matter what you are interested in, the key to mastery of the field is the ability to do your own research, to discover new facts, to evaluate and reject the superficial stuff that is readily available. You must learn to discern fact from hype, news from opinion, reality from fantasy, documentation from propaganda. This is true whether you are working with radio, television, screenwriting, Hollywood production, educational and corporate jobs, computer gaming, or interactive media.

Therefore, tell yourself that you are going to create a new personal identity, that you are going to be an independent thinker, that you are going to a new level of personal confidence and success. You are going to be a researcher! You are going to be a writer! You are going to be somebody worthy of the designation of *professional.*

The alternative is to accept that you are going to be forever a second-rate practitioner, a flunky, a perpetual gopher. Someone else is going to explore new horizons and chart new directions; you are going to do what others tell you to do. It is up to you. Read and heed what we are trying to get across in this Handbook, or admit the fact that you are destined to be a substandard scholar and mediocre hired hand.

## 2. ON UNDERSTANDING DIRECTIONS

Read and carefully re-read the explicit instructions for the writing assignments for your course. Note precisely what the instructor is asking for in matters of format (table of contents, screenplay scripting, outline, preface, appendixes, bibliography), research requirements, content, and so forth. Start by understanding clearly what it is you are supposed to be doing.

If you are uncertain about any aspect of the assignment or format, make sure you ask questions. Ask in class (other students may want to know the answers also); see your instructor during office hours. (It does little good to complain that you did not understand the assignment *after* the grade has been handed out.)

You will want to buy any models or samples of good writing recommended by your instructor—script models, sample research papers, writing handbooks, and so forth.

## 3. PLAGIARISM AND HONESTY

Colleges and universities are committed to maintaining academic integrity throughout the university community. Any form of academic dishonesty is a serious offense that can diminish the quality of scholarship, destroy the academic environment, and undermine trust and collegiality among students and instructors.

Unless a course instructor specifies that a particular assignment may be a modification or revision of some other paper or script, it is understood that *all student papers and scripts prepared for course requirements shall be original work!*

This is the specific regulation pertaining to original work for California State University, Northridge:

> Students must not allow others to conduct research or prepare any work for them without advance authorization from the instructor. This comment includes, but is not limited to, the services of commercial term paper companies. Substantial portions of the same academic work may not be submitted for credit in more than one course without authorization. . . . Students who attempt to alter and resubmit academic work with intent to defraud the faculty member will be in violation of this section.

Specific violations of the above policy include the following:

- *Plagiarism*. You cannot copy substantial segments of material from other sources (books, magazines, other papers, screenplays, the Internet, or other computer data bases) without giving the original author properly documented credit.

- *Purchase*. You only cheat yourself when you buy prepared papers or "research materials" from outside sources, *term paper mills, research companies,* or other students. You learn nothing. And you reinforce your own self-image as a fraud.

- *Recycling*. Do not submit a paper written in a previous semester to meet a current assignment for a particular course—unless the instructor makes it clear that this is acceptable.

- *Duplication*. You cannot turn in a single paper to meet different assignments in two separate courses.

- *Consultation*. Be careful when relying upon a friend, relative, or *tutor* (or paid consultant) to "correct" or "clean up" your draft.

Violation of any of the above will result in severe penalties—ranging from failing the course involved to expulsion from the University. For the full text of the Statement on Academic Dishonesty see Appendix A.

Faculty members reserve the right to pursue all reasonable methods in checking the authenticity of student papers—including review of research notes, examination of drafts of the paper or script, administration of oral exams based upon content of the paper or screenplay, and other means devised by individual instructors.

## 4. GENERAL PROCEDURES

All writing assignments follow essentially the same broad procedures. Keep these general hints in mind as you start your paper or script.

*Research Attitudes.* First comes the research—both library research and original research. No academic paper or screenplay can be created out of thin air. Start with the attitude of a dedicated scholar and professional writer/producer. Be determined that you are going to be a thorough researcher, that you are going to be honest and professional with your audience, that you will do the best possible job you can.

*Outlining.* All papers and scripts must begin with a distinct outline—either a formal academic outline or a dramatic treatment and step outline. Do not set out on any writing assignment without a clear idea of where you are headed—and how you are going to get there.

*Idea and Word Processing.* The computer is a marvelous tool for creating a document. Learn how to use the full potential of your word-processing programs. For example, start with your outline, and then simply expand, insert new content, add supporting material, and keep filling out your paper. If you have done your research and structured a solid outline, the paper or script writes itself.

*Drafting and Re-Writing.* Know that you are going to write and re-write. No first draft comes out of your printer and gets turned in. You will proceed from draft to draft. You will write, review critically, edit, re-write, and polish. No accomplished writer is satisfied with his or her early drafts. No academic paper can be considered finished after one draft is written—any more than the first draft of a screenplay is ready to be presented to the audience. The writer must examine every sentence, every thought, and continually ask himself/herself, *Is there any possible way that the reader could misinterpret what I am trying to say? Is there any way I can say this better?*

*Understanding Your Format.* Understand what is expected of you in the assignment you are undertaking. An academic paper is written for the eye; you want to maintain a formal, objective voice. A script is written for the ear; dialogue must sound natural.

*Eliminating Noise.* As a communicator, one of your primary jobs is to eliminate all communication *noise*—anything that interferes with the job of getting your message from your head into your reader's head. You want the reader to focus on your content, not stumble over your mistakes and ambiguities. This is why you must master all the elements of grammar and style: spelling, vocabulary, punctuation, capitalization, sentence structure, paragraph construction, and so forth.

*Proofreading.* After you have finished your paper or script, re-read it carefully, slowly, painstakingly. Then proofread it again. Have a friend or family member go over it for any mistakes you may not be sensitive to. (It is difficult to proofread your own work. You know what everything is supposed to say; you see what you think you wrote—an objective reader will find things that you have overlooked.) There is no excuse for turning in a paper with misspelled words, typographical mistakes, repeated phrases, omitted words, incorrect hyphenation, and other obvious flaws. You have put a lot of effort into the preparation of your paper or script; do not blow the whole thing at this point by turning in a copy that has conspicuous errors.

## 5. RESEARCH HINTS

In approaching your research, *assume an attitude of command and responsibility.* Be determined to do the best possible job you can—in order to feel good about yourself and build your sense of pride as a scholar and artist and media professional. Be as thorough and objective as possible. For any academic work, make sure you examine all sources and all sides of every issue. Do not leave yourself open to charges of bias or sloppy research. No writer, producer, or scholar ever achieved success by ignoring arguments of his or her opponents and critics.

In creating any work of fiction—short story, novel, or screenplay—thorough research is indispensable. Your imagination and personal experience can carry you only so far. Every worthwhile work of literature is based upon painstaking research. Investigate thoroughly what you are writing about—locales, characters' backgrounds, professions involved, cultures, technologies, history, bureaucracies. Do not make it up; the audience will catch any factual lapses.

### Research Sources

Utilize both library and original sources. *Library sources* may come from any organized, structured repository or storage facility: school and public libraries, corporate files, specialized collections, private compilations, government archives, and electronic data bases. They include both primary and secondary materials. *Original sources* include interviews, correspondence, questionnaires, and surveys.

For both academic writing and screenplays, you must endeavor to use the latest research available. With many topics and specialized fields, data more than a year old are as worthless as last week's weather forecasts. Check with your instructor for specific requirements and parameters, but always try to use the most recent information you can get hold of.

*Electronic Sources.* Learn how to use computer-based sources: online data bases, digital indexes and bibliographies, off-campus library catalogs, CD-ROM materials, the Internet, WWW sites, and whatever comes next. The Internet offers a wide variety of legitimate academic, corporate and government web sites, offering up-to-date data in many fields.

Be careful, however, of unsubstantiated Internet sources. For every solid piece of valid electronic information you will find on the Net, there are dozens of unsubstantiated personal sites, propaganda channels, deliberate distortions, wild fabrications, outright lies, and plenty of sloppy research, false information, and premeditated mischief. Whatever pops up on Yahoo is not the end of your research. Use your search engines with discretion.

Make sure all your Internet sources are legitimate and that all materials can be fully documented. A good rule to follow is that every item you find on the Internet should be available also in hard copy and it should have the backing of a reputable academic, corporate or government agency. Knowing how to use the Internet means knowing how to identify and discard all the distortion, hearsay, and disinformation. Check it out before you stake your reputation on it.

*Note Cards.* Use 3" x 5" note cards in your research. Jot down every individual fact, opinion, quotation, and bit of information on a separate note card (with a notation as to source). The idea is to get one item per card, so that you can later arrange and shuffle these cards as you structure your outline and fill in your supporting material. This greatly facilitates your job of analysis and synthesis.

### Use of Footnotes or Endnotes

In any formal paper, there is considerable material that you will want to explain or document in *notes*. These notes may either be *foot*notes (placed at the bottom or foot of each page) or *end*notes (placed on a separate page at the end of your text).

There are two types of notes. *Citation* notes are used to cite or document the source of a given fact, statistic, or direct quotation. In order to avoid the appearance of plagiarism, it is important to cite the author of all quotations or critical concepts. (See Appendix A, page 10, for a discussion of when to use citation notes.) It is also helpful to cite all sources for the benefit of the reader who may want to pursue a given quotation or idea. These citation notes follow a specific format for listing the author, publication, date of printing, exact pages, and other pertinent information. Make sure you follow your designated style manual (Turabian, MLA, APA) precisely in formatting these notes. See Section 9 for specific examples.

The other category of footnotes or endnotes are *explanatory* notes. These are clarifications or explanations that the author wants to insert in order to interpret or illuminate some point for the reader. They may consist of a definition, a brief historical allusion, a reference to some other matter, or any other material that the writer feels the reader may need to know. An explanatory note contains more substance than could be included in a parenthetical clause inserted in the text, but it is less substantial than an appendix added at the end of the paper.

## 6. FORMAT: THE ACADEMIC PAPER

For any academic paper, there will be specific design and appearance requirements: covers and title pages, elements to be included, page format, appendixes, and so forth. Check with your instructor to make sure you know exactly what it is you are preparing. Some considerations may include the following:

### Covers and Title Pages

Generally, short academic papers (shorter than ten pages, for example) would not ordinarily require any kind of fiber-board or plastic covers or binders. (Papers in bulky covers—which invariably differ for each student—are cumbersome to handle, read, correct, and annotate.) The pages of short research papers should be stapled in the upper left-hand corner. Larger term papers and independent research papers, however, normally would be presented in an appropriate stiff binder or set of covers. Check with your instructor as to specific requirements.

In all but the shortest papers (one or two pages), a separate title page would be appropriate. Generally, this should include the title of the assignment or report, the student's name, and the name of the course, instructor, and date submitted. Check with Turabian or other guide for the specific format.

### Front Matter

Depending on the specific assignment, a complete paper or report may include any or all of the following *front matter*: table of contents, outline, list of illustrations or charts, and preface. These items precede the content of the paper in a specific pre-arranged order (see Appendix C, page 18). These materials are all to be paginated separately, with small roman numerals—the title page would be considered page *i*; the table of contents would be page *ii* (these pages do not have the numeral actually printed on them); the outline would be page *iii*, and so forth. Arabic numerals (beginning with page *1*) are used for the text of the paper—starting with the Introduction. (Note the pagination of the beginning pages in this Handbook.)

*Table of Contents*. Any paper of substantial length should have a table of contents (see page 18). The function of this page is to itemize all of the main sections of the pa-

per (outline, list of illustrations, preface, introduction, main points, conclusion, endnotes, bibliography, other appendixes) and the page number where each section starts. This is not an outline, so detailed subdivisions of the body of the paper are not appropriate—just the main headings are needed. The table of contents is, in essence, a directory to help the reader find the various segments of the paper.

*Outline*. Many instructors will also want a formal outline preceding a comprehensive paper or report. This would immediately follow the table of contents, identified as page *iii*. (See Section 8 on procedures for creating the outline and page 19 for a sample outline.)

*List of Figures or Illustrations*. The content of many papers often can be presented more clearly in charts, models, figures, illustrations, tables, and other visual displays. As a media student, you are, after all, concerned with visual communication; do not overlook the value of graphic presentations in your paper. Such materials—if extensive—should be numbered and have a separate listing in the table of contents (as page *iv*).

### End Matter

Following the conclusion of the text of your paper, there are several items of *end matter* that may be included. All of the end-matter pages continue with the Arabic numeral pagination.

*Endnotes*. If you have not included *footnotes* at the bottom (or *foot*) of each page throughout the paper, you will have your citations listed as *endnotes* at the end of your paper. These would be numbered notes on a separate page or pages immediately following your text.

*Appendixes*. Although student papers would not usually include end matter such as a glossary or an index, there are often instances when you would want to include one or more appendixes. These would be various kinds of materials which may be of interest to the reader, although they are not crucial enough to be incorporated as an integral part of the body of the paper. Appendixes would include items such as expanded illustrations, historical summaries, statistical tables, maps, case studies, legal documents, and other interesting tangential items.

*Bibliography*. The final item in most academic papers would be a Bibliography or "References" section. Some instructors may specify that you should include only those works (books, journals, magazines, newspapers, government reports, pamphlets, Internet materials, audio and visual sources) that you actually cited in the paper. Others may want you to include every item that you consulted in the preparation of your paper. Some instructors may ask only for the listing of the materials referred to; others may ask for an *annotation* of each item—a brief summary or evaluation of each work. Make sure you understand what is requested for your particular assignment. And make sure you follow the proper style manual specified by your instructor (see Section 9).

## Section Headings

In between the front matter and end matter you will present the text of your paper—often divided into an Introduction, Body, and Conclusion.

In order to make your paper as readable as possible, you will want to consider using various levels of headings. (This also will make your paper look more appealing and easier to follow.) Corresponding usually to the divisions of your outline, these headings normally would not be identified by numbers (although they might be in a larger work). Several different levels of subordination can be implied just by the placement and spacing of various headings. Word processing software will allow you to make headings stand out with different type faces, font sizes, and use of boldface and/or italics.

In this Handbook, for example, three different orders of headings have been used: the **upper-case centered section heading** (e.g., "6. FORMAT: THE ACADEMIC PAPER"); the **margin heading with initial caps** (e.g., "Front Matter"); and the ***italicized boldface paragraph heading*** (e.g., "List of Figures or Illustrations"). Be creative and experiment with differing formats; just be careful not to overdo it and wind up with a pretentious mixture that distracts from the content of your paper.

In Appendix C, page 20, you will find a sample of a properly formatted page for an academic paper. Look it over carefully and read the annotations incorporated between the lines. Note how various levels of section headings are used. (Note also the warning against justifying the right margin.)

## 7. FORMAT: SCRIPTS AND SCREENPLAYS

As with academic papers, there are very precise format requirements for scripts. These formats will vary according to specific assignments and medium considerations. You may be required to follow precisely the format for any one of several different scripting jobs: screenplay, teleplay, situation comedy, television script (single column or double column), radio or audio-only script, industrial or corporate script, and other specific professional assignments. Make sure you understand clearly from your instructor exactly which format to follow; make sure you have the proper model to guide you.

## The Cover Page

The cover or title page of any script should contain the script title, your name, course, date, and professor's name.

For most script projects, you will be required to turn in your script on three-holed paper. The script should not be stapled or presented in a bound format. The pages should be held together by brads.

## Specific Format Requirements

Format specifications and details will differ from medium to medium. For each particular script format there will be very specific requirements regarding the use of columns, margins, upper and lower case letters, indentations, placement of characters' names, stage directions, camera instructions, and so forth. Check with your instructor and make sure you follow the given instructions precisely.

In any professional situation, the very first impression you will make (as a writer) is what your script looks like. Some script reader, producer, director, studio head, or assistant is going to look at your work and immediately form an initial impression—*either* "This person knows what he or she is doing" *or* "This person really hasn't a clue." Format matters.

## Supplemental Materials

For most scripting assignments, you will also be required to turn in supplemental materials. Just as an outline is an absolute prerequisite before writing an academic paper, so are certain preparatory materials needed before you can complete any kind of script. You may be required to prepare any or all of the following: a log line, a premise, a step outline, and/or a treatment. Make sure you thoroughly understand the assignment and your instructor's directions before proceeding with the script.

## Sample Script Pages

Appendix D contains annotated *templates* for both a film and a situation comedy, plus sample page formats for a one-column TV script, a two-column TV script, a film screenplay, an instructional film, a radio script, and one page of another screenplay. A two-page Premise is also included. Look these over carefully and read the annotations incorporated in each sample.

## 8. OUTLINING

Just as a premise, treatment, and step outline are required for any script project, so is a solid organizational approach expected in any research paper. In fact, in any kind of media presentation—academic paper, documentary film, educational video, speech to the PTA—it is imperative that you begin with a clear well-structured outline.

Often an explicit organizational pattern may be specified by your instructor for a particular assignment—

comparison-contrast, topical arrangement, case study, field study, modified thesis, and so forth. In other cases, a problem-solution approach would be appropriate. In all cases the writer should follow a pattern of data *analysis* (in examining the subject) and data *synthesis* (in structuring the content).

In writing any paper, the author must start with a clear, carefully constructed outline. The outline serves as the blueprint for the paper. Writing a paper without an outline (planning to construct the outline after completing the paper, in order to satisfy an academic requirement) is like building a house with no plans (and then drawing up the blueprints after the house is finished, to satisfy the county planning department).

The outline is integral to solid planning and clear thinking throughout the entire writing process. Whether or not the outline is turned in (depending upon the instructor's directions), the writer must construct the outline before attempting to write the paper. Once you have finished a proper outline, you are now ready to finish writing the paper. Just fill in the subpoints and supporting material and the paper writes itself.

Appendix B, page 12, includes a summary of sixteen guidelines for the proper formatting of an academic outline. Appendix C, page 19, illustrates a completed outline.

## 9. MATTERS OF STYLE

In writing any academic paper or script, there are certain style guidelines and rules that must be followed. You have to pay close attention to these conventions.

### Style Manuals

First of all, check with your instructor to determine what specific style format is desired (or required). Although there may be specific instances when an instructor might designate some other specific format, most of the time one of the following three manuals would be appropriate for academic subjects in media studies.

- The University of Chicago Style Manual, as summarized in Turabian's *A Manual for Writers of Term Papers, Theses, and Dissertations.*

- The Modern Language Association style, as summarized in the *MLA Handbook for Writers of Research Papers.*

- The APA style, as summarized in the *Publication Manual of the American Psychological Association.*

Full bibliographic references for these three manuals are included in the Bibliography at the end of this Writing Handbook (page 35). If no specific style is designated, consider the Chicago Style Manual (Turabian) to be the default format to follow. In the case of any uncertainties or ambiguities, *always check with your instructor.*

Any of these three manuals will cover all questions of style and format that you will normally need to follow: pagination, margins, spacing, outlining, abbreviations, use of numerals, footnotes, bibliographies, and similar matters. They also provide invaluable information and guidelines in the creative and academic aspects of preparing a satisfactory paper: selecting a topic, library usage, research sources and approaches, style and tone, stating a purpose, draft revisions, and other areas.

### Formats for Notes and Bibliography

Pay particular attention to the proper format for notes (footnotes or endnotes) and bibliographic citations. Notes and bibliographic entries are not formatted in the same manner. They vary as to the author's name, punctuation, and other information to be included. Note the distinctions, for example, in how the Chicago style (Turabian) distinguishes between notes and bibliography:

*Note*

> [5]Jacques Ellul, *The Technological Society*, trans. John Wilkinson (New York: Vintage Books, 1964), pp. 58-59.

*Bibliography*

> Ellul, Jacques. *The Technological Society*. Translated by John Wilkinson. New York: Vintage Books, 1964.

The MLA and APA formats make similar distinctions between notes and bibliographies.

Appendix C, page 21, illustrates some distinctions among Turabian, MLA, and APA bibliographic formats.

*Internet Citations.* When using material from electronic sources, several other formatting factors must be considered. First of all, the source of the data will dictate the specific format—whether the material comes from World Wide Web (WWW) sites, File Transfer Protocol (FTP) sites, e-mail, listserv messages, newsgroupups, chat rooms, or other synchronous communications. As mentioned in Section 5, many of these sources may be quite questionable and transitory. As with printed sources, there are also slight differences between the Chicago style, MLA and APA formats when it comes to Internet documentation. Several of the materials listed in the "Electronic Citations" section of the Bibliography (page 36) will illustrate those distinctions.

Care must be taken in citing Internet sources. For example, you may need to note both the date of an original document as well as the date when it was posted or when you retrieved it; you must consider both the location of the original material and the address where it was posted. As with printed materials, you must be concerned with two things: validating the source to the satisfaction of your reader, and giving the reader whatever information is needed so that he or she may consult the source for further reference.

Listed below are typical examples of a format for both a note citation and a bibliographic reference.

*Note (Chicago Manual of Style format)*

```
⁷Brian Kehoe, Zen and the Art of the
Internet, 2d ed. (1992). Available
[Online]: <ftp://quake.think.com/pub/
etext/1992/zen10.txt> [25 March
1995].
```

***Bibliography (MLA format)***

```
Kehoe, Brian P. 1992. Zen and the art
of the Internet. 2d ed. Available
[Online]: <ftp://quake.think.com/
pub/etext/1992/zen10.txt> [25 March
1995].
```

Note the use of pointed brackets < . . . > to designate the beginning and close of any Internet address. Wherever you have enough room, you should include the entire Internet address all on one line.

There are several good sources (available on the Internet) for electronic citations. Three of them are listed below:

<http://www.people.memphis.edu/~mcrouse/elcite.html>
Authored by Maurice Crouse of the University of Memphis, this is a good comprehensive investigation of Internet citations.

<http://h-net.msu.edu/~africa/citation.html>
Compiled by Melvin Page of the University of Natal at Durban, South Africa, this overview focuses on the Chicago Style Manual format.

<http://english.ttu.edu/kairos/inbox/1.2/mla_archive.html>
For MLA users, this is a very thorough article written by Andrew Harnack and Gene Kleppinger of Eastern Kentucky University.

## Other Stylistic Concerns

In addition to the above items (and related factors covered earlier in this Handbook), there are other matters of style you should be aware of—pertaining to spacing, margins, spelling out of numbers, underlining and italicizing titles, abbreviations, contractions, acronyms, hyphenation, apostrophes, and so forth. Appendix B lists a few of these stylistic concerns—specifically pages 13 and 14. Various style manuals and writing handbooks mentioned in

the Bibliography will illustrate many other stylistic and printing conventions you should be comfortable with.

## 10. WRITING TIPS

College students should be able to demonstrate proper use of the English language: paragraph construction, sentence structure, spelling, good word choice, correct grammar, capitalization, punctuation, and so forth. No student should plan on trying to complete a major in any media field without demonstrating mastery of the written language expected of an educated person.

Students with noticeable deficiencies in the ability to use the written language should consult manuals on writing and English usage. Several are listed in the Bibliography. Other books are available in the "References" section of your college bookstore. Students with serious writing problems should investigate writing programs offered by a campus learning center, English as a Second Language Laboratory, or remedial programs offered by the English Department. Check with your academic advisor or the counseling center for other resources.

Even the best of writers will occasionally have trouble with a few common grammatical and stylistic problems. Appendix B lists a few major considerations you should be aware of. There are many other basic rules concerning verb tense, agreement of subject and verb, adverbial construction, punctuation, capitalization, sentence structure, and so forth. Buy a good reference manual and use it.

In fact, as a writer, when working on any script or research paper, you should have at your elbow—in addition to any on-line resources—a dictionary, a thesaurus, the latest edition of a world almanac, a writing handbook, and a style manual.

## 11. APPEARANCE

For both research papers and scripts, you want your finished product to look as professional as possible. Papers should be clean and free from any obvious blemishes. Part of your concern as a media major should be the packaging of all visual presentations—including written papers—as neatly and attractively as you can.

### Copy Quality

All academic papers must be typewritten or computer-printed. Use heavy weight printing or typing paper—at least 16-pound. Normally, instructors will specify that they want the original copy turned in; try to submit a paper that does not have excessive erasures or amounts of correction fluid. Some instructors, on the other hand, may request neat photocopies. In this case, make sure that the copies are on white bond paper and are clean and free of dingy background. (Some instructors may require that you turn in both the original and a photocopy, the latter to remain in their files.)

If you do find errors in the paper at the last minute (and cannot reprint the document), make all corrections neatly in ink. It is better to turn in a paper with neat corrections than to turn in a copy with mistakes—hoping that the reader does not find them.

(In all instances, make sure you keep a copy of any paper or script turned in for any course assignment. This is a good practice to observe in all academic and professional situations.)

## Acceptable Fonts

In selecting a typeface for your computer-printing job, make sure that you use a conventional font and type size. Courier (simulating typewriter print) is, of course, acceptable and, in fact, is preferred for most script assignments. Other suitable fonts include Times Roman, CG Times, Dutch 801, Roman-WP, Century PS, Times New Roman, Bookman Old Style, Century Schoolbook, Tiempo, and similar Roman *serif* fonts. Less desirable are *sans serif* fonts such as Helvitica, Century Gothic, Arial, Letter Gothic, Universe, Geneva, and the like—although these fonts may be useful for section headings and other material such as tables and charts. By all means avoid any fancy or artistic fonts. (For the information of the reader, this Handbook was printed in 10-point Times New Roman; headings were Arial.) The objective is to make the paper as readable as possible—to avoid communication noise; fonts should not call attention to themselves.

Check with your instructor as to acceptable type sizes. Unless otherwise approved, you should probably stick to 12-point type. In Courier, this may be designated as "10-cpi" *(characters-per-inch)* or *Pica*. Some instructors may permit 11-point or even 10-point. For footnotes or explanatory matter in tables, you may want to use 10-point or even 9-point.

Again, the key is to turn in as professional a copy as possible. Packaging your media presentation is crucial to academic and professional success.

# APPENDIX A

CSUN Statement on Academic Dishonesty
(including reference to Section 41301 of the
*California Administrative Code)*

# UNIVERSITY STATEMENT ON ACADEMIC DISHONESTY

The maintenance of academic integrity and quality education is the responsibility of each student at California State University, Northridge. Cheating or plagiarism in connection with an academic program is listed in Section 41301, Title 5, *California Code of Regulations*, as an offense for which a student may be expelled, suspended, or given a less severe disciplinary sanction.

Academic dishonesty is an especially serious offense and diminishes the quality of scholarship and defrauds those who depend upon the integrity of the campus programs. Such dishonesty includes the following:

## A. CHEATING

Intentionally using or attempting to use unauthorized materials, information, or study aids in any academic exercise.

*Comments:*

1. Faculty members are encouraged to state in advance their policies and procedures concerning examinations and other academic exercises as well as the use before examinations of shared study aids, examination files, and other related materials and forms of assistance.
2. Students completing any examination should assume that external assistance (e.g., books, notes, calculators, conversation with others) is prohibited unless specifically authorized by the instructor.
3. Students must not allow others to conduct research or prepare any work for them without advance authorization from the instructor. This includes, but is not limited to, the services of commercial term paper companies.
4. Substantial portions of the same academic work may not be submitted for credit in more than one course without authorization.

## B. FABRICATION

Intentional fabrication or invention of any information or citation in an academic exercise.

*Comments:*

1. "Invented" information may not be used in any laboratory experiment or other academic exercise without notice to and authorization from the instructor.
2. One should acknowledge reliance upon the actual source from which cited information was obtained. For example, a writer should not reproduce a quotation from a book review and indicate that the quotation was obtained from the book itself.
3. Students who attempt to alter and resubmit academic work with intent to defraud the faculty member will be in violation of this section. For example, a student may not change an answer on a returned exam and then claim that they [sic] deserve additional credit.

## C. FACILITATING ACADEMIC DISHONESTY

Intentionally or knowingly helping or attempting to help another to commit an act of academic dishonesty.

*Comment:*

For example, one who knowingly allowed another to copy from his or her paper during an examination would be in violation of this section.

## D. PLAGIARISM

Intentionally or knowingly representing the words, ideas, or work of another as one's own in any academic exercise.

*Comments:*

1. **Direct Quotation**: Every direct quotation must be identified by quotation marks, or by appropriate indentation or by other means of identification, and must be promptly cited in a footnote. Proper footnote style for any academic department is outlined by the *MLA Style Sheet* or K. L. Turabian's *A Manual for Writers of Term Papers, Theses and Dissertations.* These and similar publications are available in the Matador Bookstore and at the Reference Desk at the Oviatt Library.
2. **Paraphrase**: Prompt acknowledgment is required when material from another source is paraphrased or summarized in whole or in part in your own words. To acknowledge a paraphrase properly, one might state: "to paraphrase Locke's comment . . ." and conclude with a footnote identifying the exact reference. A footnote acknowledging only a directly quoted statement does not suffice to notify the reader of any preceding or succeeding paraphrased material.
3. **Borrowed Facts or Information**: Information obtained in one's reading or research which is not common knowledge among students in the course must be acknowledged. Examples of common knowledge might include the names of leaders of prominent nations, basic scientific laws, etc. Materials which contribute only to one's general understanding of the subject may be acknowledged in the bibliography and need not be immediately footnoted. One footnote is usually sufficient to acknowledge indebtedness when a number of connected sentences in the paper draw their special information from one source. When direct quotations are used, however, quotation marks must be inserted and prompt acknowledgment is required.

## FACULTY POLICY ON ACADEMIC DISHONESTY

Depending upon the severity of the offense and the student's disciplinary history as it relates to acts of academic dishonesty, the faculty member may elect to exercise the following options:

1. Assign a lower or failing grade to an assignment, examination, or the entire course. In cases in which the faculty member elects to exercise the grade penalty option, the faculty member must inform the student in a timely manner that academic dishonesty was a factor in the evaluation. In cases where the sanction for an act of academic dishonesty has been the assignment of a grade penalty without a simultaneous request for formal disciplinary action and in which the student wishes to challenge the grade penalty assigned, the student may file an appeal with the Academic Grievance and Grade Appeals Board. (Forms are available in the Office of the Vice President for Student Affairs.)
2. Request that the Office of the Vice President for Student Affairs notify the student that information related to the student's alleged act of academic dishonesty within that particular class has been received. Such notifications are in the form of an admonitory letter and serve to inform the student that the Office of Vice President for Student Affairs is aware of the alleged incident and that formal disciplinary action will not be taken.
3. Request disciplinary action against the student. Student discipline is exclusively the province of the Office of the Vice President for Student Affairs. In such cases, the faculty member, through the department chair and school dean, should submit a formal written report of the incident to the Assistant Vice President for Student Life and request formal disciplinary action.

## PENALTIES

Section 41301, Title 5, *California Code of Regulations*, as published in the University Catalog, Appendix I, provides that a student may be expelled, suspended, placed on probation, or given a lesser sanction for a proven violation of the Student Conduct Code. Among the violations listed in Section 41301, cheating or plagiarism in connection with an academic program is specifically included.

# APPENDIX  B

Miscellaneous Materials and Writing Guidelines

- Outline Format: Guidelines
- Some Stylistic Concerns
- A Few Grammatical and Punctuation Considerations
- "29 Rules for Righting a Good Reserch Paper"

# Outline Format: Guidelines

Unless given other specific instructions, the following guidelines should be followed in constructing your outline. This format would be appropriate for all academic papers.

1. The outline will consist of five segments: **Purpose**; **Thesis** or summary statement; **Introduction**; **Body**; and **Conclusion**.

2. The Purpose will begin with an infinitive phrase (*such as* "To examine . . ." *or* "To convince . . .").

3. The Thesis (summary statement) is a one-sentence summary of your presentation; it is a declarative and more specific reiteration of your Purpose. It will translate directly into the main points of your Body.

4. The Introduction gives your audience the *preparation* it needs for the Body of your presentation. It will be divided into subsections designated by upper-case, or capital, letters (*A, B, C*).

5. The Conclusion will wrap up your presentation with either a *Summary* or an *Appeal to action* (or both). It also will be divided into subsections designated by upper-case letters.

6. The Body will consist of *two to five main points.*

7. The main points will be clear divisions of your Thesis.

8. The main points must be logically coordinated. They will be **Totally Inclusive** (taken together the main points must cover the whole topic) and **Mutually Exclusive** (the main points must be distinct— no overlapping).

9. Use **parallel wording** for the main points to show their logical relationships.

10. The main points will follow some clear and logical pattern: chronological, spatial, topical, or other classification.

11. The main points will be designated by Roman numerals (*I, II, III, IV*). Labeling of main points is the only place in the outline where you will use **Roman numerals**.

12. The main points will be divided into logical and subordinate subpoints. These subpoints (like the divisions of the Introduction and Conclusion) will use upper-case letters.

13. Use proper indentation for each division and subpoint.

14. All subordinate divisions will use proper labels (Arabic numerals, lower-case letters, small Roman numerals, and so forth).

15. There must be at least *two divisions* (or subdivisions) for each point that is divided—at any level.

16. Every main point (and subpoint) must be a **full sentence**.

# Some Stylistic Concerns

1.  Double-space all text—except for long quotations, footnotes or endnotes, and bibliographic entries.

2.  Watch your margins; generally leave one inch on both sides and at the top and bottom of each page.

3.  Check Turabian or other style manual on the proper spelling out of numbers. Generally spell out all numbers smaller than one hundred. Other manuals say you should spell out all numbers that can be written with one or two words. Never start a sentence with numerals.

4.  Always <u>underline</u> (or *italicize*) the titles of major works: names of books, magazines, newspapers, films, and television series. Use "quotation marks" for subordinate divisions—chapter titles, articles, individual programs in a TV series. For example: `The program, "The Soup Nazi," was one of the more popular episodes of` <u>`Seinfeld`</u>`.`

5.  Generally avoid all abbreviations in an academic paper.

6.  Whenever you hyphenate a word, make sure you have a proper break between syllables.

7.  Write out `"percent"` and `"and"` rather than use the symbols, % and &.

8.  Contractions are not to be used in a formal academic paper (`can't`, `won't`, `doesn't`, `you'll`, `should've`, and so forth).

9.  The use of *`it's`* is not appropriate. (*`It's`* is a contraction; the possessive form of the pronoun *`it`* simply is *`its`*.)

10. The abbreviation `"T.V."` is not acceptable. If you must use an abbreviation, *TV* is acceptable.

11. Acronyms can be used only after the full term has been spelled out. Example: `"The Audit Bureau of Circulations (ABC) plays an important role."`

12. Use the apostrophe correctly to indicate the possessive case. `"There were three` ***`countries`*** `involved. The citizens of Canada were concerned with their` ***`country's`*** `security. But we must consider all three` ***`countries'`*** `existing treaties."`

13. Do not omit the possessive apostrophe where it should be used. *`"Today's`* `programming chiefs must consider` ***`children's`*** `needs."`

14. Use the hyphen for compound modifiers. `"The` **`one-hour`** `newscast included two` **`gang-related`** `stories dealing with` **`inner-city`** `youths and the` **`drop-out`** `problem."`

15. Use the double-hyphen for a dash. `"The correct way of using the dash--which is a convenient form of punctuation--is to use two hyphens with no space on either side."`

16. Leave spaces between *ellipsis* dots, for example, `"whenever you use them to indicate the omission of . . . material from a quotation."`

# A Few Grammatical and Punctuation Considerations

1. Generally avoid the use of first-person pronouns ("I," "my," "me") in all academic papers and research reports.

2. Do not use the second person ("you") when referring to people in general; use the third person. Instead of writing, "As a viewer, you should be aware of . . ." *write,* "As a viewer, a person should be aware of . . ."

3. Do not use "he" or "him" as an indefinite, universal pronoun (standing in for "producer" or "doctor"). Use a gender-neutral construction such as "he/she" or "he or she."

4. Do not use a plural pronoun such as "they/them/their" without a proper plural antecedent. (Note that the *FCC, network, family,* and *court* are all singular nouns.)

5. Always use words such as "criteria," "media," or "data" as plural nouns. *Wrong:* The data shows that each media should have a criteria. *Correct:* The data show that each medium should have at least one criterion.

6. Learn how to use *whom* correctly—as the object of a preposition or a verb. "This report is written for whom?" "Whom can we turn to?" "She hit whom?"

7. Remember that "fewer" refers to a quantity that can be counted; "less" refers to a non-quantifiable noun. There were fewer incidents of violence on TV this year; this means there is less mayhem being depicted.

8. Similarly, with "number" (which can be counted) and "amount" (which cannot be quantified). The number of murders went down; but there was a greater amount of unnecessary violence.

9. Be careful with homophones: there/their/they're; hear/here; sight/site/cite; to/too/two; whose/who's; and so forth.

10. Be especially careful with words that are "near-homophones." Three specific troublesome examples are affect/effect, than/then, and our/are.

11. Always leave two spaces after the end of each and every sentence. Then you begin a new sentence.

12. Placing a period outside of closing quotation marks is not acceptable. *Wrong:* The boy said "Hogwash". *Correct:* The boy said "Hogwash." Generally, the same is true for commas.

13. Use the *colon* only at the end of an independent clause—never immediately following a verb. *Wrong:* The three theories are: catharsis, modeling, and desensitization. *Correct:* There are three theories: catharsis, modeling, and desensitization.

14. Footnote (endnote) numerals in the text should be *superscript* numerals (small numerals placed above the line); they should come after the terminal sentence punctuation and any closing quotation marks. "This is an example of how they should be placed."[23]

15. Avoid using "etc." Use some construction such as "and so forth."

# "29 RULES FOR RIGHTING A GOOD RESEARCH PAPER"

Culled from a variety of sources, here are some delightful tongue-in-cheek examples of what *NOT* to do.

1. Each pronoun should agree with their antecedent.
2. I always avoid first-person pronouns in my formal papers.
3. Just between you and I, case is important.
4. Its important to use you're apostrophe's correctly.
5. A papers quality depends upon it's use of the possessive case.
6. Verbs has to agree with their subjects.
7. Their is a need to beware of homonyms and there different spellings.
8. Spel correckly --especialy when discussing a stashun's frekwency.
9. When evaluating a media, you must use several criterias.
10. Don't use no double negatives. Not never.
11. One shouldn't use contractions because they don't belong in a formal paper.
12. A writer should not shift your point of view when talking about people in general--especially oneself.
13. Don't write a run-on sentence you have got to punctuate it other wise it is hard to read.
14. No sentence fragments. Not in a formal paper.
15. In reports and papers use commas to keep things nouns and verbs separated without which we would have without doubt confusion.
16. But, do not use, commas, which are not necessary.
17. Do not abbreviate unless absolutely nec. to make a comm. report more readable for a nat'l audience.
18. As far as incomplete construction, it is wrong.
19. Try to write careful, adverbwise.
20. Avoid clichés like the plague.
21. Always avoid awkward, affected alliteration.
22. Be more or less specific.
23. And try never to start a sentence with a conjunction.
24. Do not overuse exclamation marks!!!
25. Avoid un-necessary hyphens.
26. You've probably heard it a million times--resist hyperbole and overstatement.
27. Exaggeration is a billion times worse than understatement.
28. Check carefully to see if you any words out.
29. About repetition, the repetition of a word is not usually effective repetition.
30. Reread and edit your writing and you will find upon rereading and editing that a great deal of repetition and redundancy of phrases used over and over again can be avoided through this rereading and editing.

# APPENDIX C

Sample Materials for an Academic Paper

- Sample Table of Contents
- Sample Outline for Academic Paper
- Sample Page of Academic Paper
- Sample Bibliographic Formats

*[Sample Table of Contents ]*

# CONTENTS

Page

Outline . . . . . . . . . . . . . . . . . . . . . . . iii

*[Note that the right margin has the last number vertically aligned ]*

List of Illustrations . . . . . . . . . . . . . . . . iv

*[Note that the dots leading from heading to page number are spaced and are vertically aligned ]*

List of Charts . . . . . . . . . . . . . . . . . . . v

Preface . . . . . . . . . . . . . . . . . . . . . vi

Introduction . . . . . . . . . . . . . . . . . . . 1

   I. Converting Main Points *[This is the first main point of the Body ]* . . . . . . 3

  II. Purpose and Thesis *[Second main point ]* . . . . . . . . . . . 4

III. Pattern for Main Points *[Third main point ]* . . . . . . . . . . 6

 IV. Filling in the Outline *[Fourth main point ]* . . . . . . . . . . 7

  V. Conclusion and Introduction *[Fifth main point ]* . . . . . . . . . 9

Conclusion . . . . . . . . . . . . . . . . . . . 10

Endnotes . . . . . . . . . . . . . . . . . . . 12

Appendix A. Statement on Academic Honesty . . . . . . . . . 13

Appendix B. Miscellaneous Guidelines . . . . . . . . . . . 14

Appendix C. Sample Materials . . . . . . . . . . . . . 17

Appendix D. Script Formats . . . . . . . . . . . . . . 20

Glossary . . . . . . . . . . . . . . . . . . . . 24

Bibliography . . . . . . . . . . . . . . . . . . 26

## TOPIC: PREPARING AN OUTLINE

**PURPOSE:** To illustrate the five steps involved in preparing any kind of academic or media outline.

*[Your one-sentence "thesis" should parallel what you indicated in your Purpose ]*

**THESIS:** There are five steps involved in the preparation of an academic or media outline.

*[Your Thesis should divide clearly and logically into the Main Points of the Body ]*

### INTRODUCTION

    A. The purpose of the outline must be understood.
    B. A distinction must be made between information and persuasion.
    C. The overall structure includes five components.

*[Lettered divisions of Introduction and Conclusion should be aligned with subpoints in the Body ]*

### BODY

  I. The first step is converting your Topic Analysis into the main points of your outline.
    A. Review the eight "Patterns of Translation."
    B. Select one segment of your Topic Analysis to be converted into your main points.
    C. Confirm which of the eight patterns you will use.
    D. Tentatively, determine the use for the rest of your Topic Analysis.
      1. Conclusion.
      2. Introduction.

*[Note parallel wording of the main points ]*

 II. The second step is writing your Purpose and Thesis.
    A. The Purpose must be an infinitive phrase.
      1. It must include only one single idea.
      2. It must conform to your Thesis.
    B. The Thesis is a summary of your one point or proposition.
      1. It must be a single sentence.
      2. It must divide clearly into your main points.

III. The third step is selecting a structured pattern for main points.
    A. One approach is chronological.
    B. A second approach is spatial.
    C. A third approach is categorical or topical.
    D. A fourth approach is classification or taxonomical.
    E. Another approach is a variation of problem-solving.

 IV. The fourth step is editing and filling in the outline.

  V. The fifth step is writing the remainder of your outline.
    A. The Conclusion includes cognitive and affective components.
    B. The Introduction includes cognitive and affective components.

### CONCLUSION

    A. There are several format requirements to consider.
      1. Main points and subpoints must be properly indented.
      2. Points must be properly labeled.
        a. Use Roman numerals for main points.
        b. Use upper case letters for subpoints.
      3. You should have two to five main points.
      4. Use full sentences for main points and subpoints.
      5. Use obvious, redundant, parallel wording for main points.
      6. Use proper coordination and subordination.

    B. Type and proofread your outline carefully.

# SAMPLE SECTION (FIRST-LEVEL) HEADING

This page is set in Courier 11-point font. Check with your

*[Note the use of double-spacing throughout]*

instructor to see what fonts are acceptable. Normally it looks better if you include some text before going to the next level heading.

*[You may want to leave an additional space before the next heading]*

## Sample Sub-Section (Second-Level) Heading

The second-level heading would typically follow the subpoints of your outline. You may leave an additional space (triple-space) before the heading. Note that the heading can be an abbreviated phrase; the outline itself should be full sentences.

*[Note that you may also want to leave an extra space before the Margin Heading]*

### Margin Headings

The margin heading is flush with the left-hand margin. It indicates a subdivision of your second-level heading. The more you take advantage of using various levels of headings, the easier it is for the reader to follow the content and organization of your paper.

*Paragraph Heading.* This is a paragraph heading--which is the lowest level of heading you would use. Note that it is both **boldface** and *italicized*. Instead of using italics, you may want to underline this paragraph heading. Make sure that it stands out so that it will not be mistaken for a sentence fragment. This paragraph is "justified"--that is, the right-hand margin is vertically aligned so that you have a straight line down the right-hand margin. It may look neat, but it also can result in awkward spacing, especially if you have text with exceptionally large words. Therefore, various instructors emphatically may tell you not to use the justification feature of your printer. Generally speaking, unjustified text is easier to read.

One other stylistic item: never leave a heading "widowed" at the bottom of a page with no text following it. Use a forced page break to put the heading at the top of the next page.

### WIDOWED SECTION HEADING   *[This looks pretty lame]*

## University of Chicago Press (Turabian)

DeFleur, Melvin L., and Ball-Rokeach, Sandra. <u>Theories of Mass
Communication</u>. 5th ed. New York: Longman, 1989.

Lasswell, Harold D. "The Structure and Function of Communication in
Society." In <u>The Communication of Ideas</u>, edited by Lyman Bronson.
New York: Harper & Brothers, 1948.

Rosenberg, Bernard, and White, David Manning, eds. <u>Mass Culture</u>.
Glencoe, IL: Free Press, 1957.

*[Journal entry ]*
Sapolsky, Barry S., and Tabarlet, Joseph O. "Sex in Primetime
Television: 1979 Versus 1989." <u>Journal of Broadcasting and
Electronic Media</u> , 35, no. 4 (Fall 1991): 505-16.

*[Popular magazine ]*
Turque, Bill. "Picking a Fight About the Future." <u>Newsweek</u>, 9 December
1996, pp. 30-31.

## MLA (Modern Language Association)

DeFleur, Melvin L., and Sandra Ball-Rokeach. <u>Theories of Mass
Communication</u>. 5th ed. New York: Longman, 1989.

Lasswell, Harold D. "The Structure and Function of Communication in
Society." In <u>The Communication of Ideas</u>. Ed. Lyman Bronson.
New York: Harper & Brothers, 1948, pp. 145-78.

Rosenberg, Bernard, and David Manning White, eds. <u>Mass Culture</u>.
Glencoe, IL: Free Press, 1957.

Sapolsky, Barry S., and Joseph O. Tabarlet. "Sex in Primetime
Television: 1979 Versus 1989." <u>Journal of Broadcasting and
Electronic Media</u>, 35, No. 4 (Fall 1991), 505-16.

Turque, Bill. "Picking a Fight About the Future." <u>Newsweek</u>, 9 Dec. 1996,
pp. 30-31.

## APA (American Psychological Association)

DeFleur, M. L., & Ball-Rokeach, S. (1989). <u>Theories of mass
communication</u> (5th ed.). New York: Longman.

Lasswell, H. D. (1948). The structure and function of communication in
society. In Lyman Bronson (Ed.), <u>Communication of Ideas</u> (pp.
145-78). New York: Harper & Brothers.

Rosenberg, B., & White, D. M. (Eds.). (1957). <u>Mass culture</u>.
Glencoe, IL: Free Press.

Sapolsky, B. S., & Tabarlet, J. O. (1991). Sex in primetime
television: 1979 versus 1989. <u>Journal of Broadcasting and
Electronic Media</u>, 35 (4), 505-16.

Turque, B. (1996, December 9). Picking a fight about the future.
<u>Newsweek</u>, CXXVIII (24), 30-31.

# APPENDIX  D

Sample Materials for Script Formats

- Film Format Template *[Annotated ]*

- Situation Comedy Template *[Annotated]*

- Sample Script: Single-Column Television *

- Sample Script: Two-Column Television *

- Sample Script: Teleplay/Screenplay *

- Sample Script: Instructional Film *

- Sample Radio Script

- Script Excerpt

- Sample Premise

FADE IN:
*[Double space]*
INT. [*or* EXT.]    LOCATION or SUBJECT - DAY [*or* NIGHT]    *[slug line or banner head]*
*[Double space]*
Description of scenes, characters, and action are typed across
the page.  When <u>first</u> introduced, character names are
CAPITALIZED.  References to camera movement, music, and/or sound
effects are also CAPITALIZED.                    *[Description of action]*
*[Double space]*

                         CHARACTER                    *[Character name]*
                 (manner in which the          *[parenthetical or*
                  character speaks)             *directional cue]*
            The actual line of dialogue goes here.    *[dialogue]*
                  (beat)                              *[parenthetical]*
            Parenthetical directions are on separate line.
*[double space]*

                      SECOND CHARACTER
            Speaks here.
*[double space]*
If there is a break in the dialogue before another character
speaks, then:
*[double space]*

                      SECOND CHARACTER
                 (continuing)
            Completes his/her speech in this manner.
*[double space]*
Additional descriptions of action and CAMERA MOVEMENTS are typed
in this manner, as needed.

[MASTER SCENE FORMAT: Writer is concerned with the basic slug
line, concise descriptions of action and dialogue.  Detailed
camera moves or shot descriptions are usually NOT included.  When
the writer describes camera set-ups, it is preferable to use
*generic* descriptions such as ANGLE ON . . ., CAMERA FOLLOWS
. . ., CAMERA MOVES IN . . ., etc.  Early drafts rarely include
directions like RACK FOCUS TO . . ., ZOOM IN ON . . ., CRANE UP
. . ., etc.]
                                        TRANSITIONS GO HERE
*[e.g.,* DISSOLVE TO:, WIPE TO:, *etc.* A CUT *is otherwise assumed]*
                      CHARACTER
            When the speech of a character is so long
            that it must go beyond its initial page,
            then it may be . . .
                 (MORE)      *[refers to the dialogue]*
*[double space]*


                                   CONTINUED  *[refers to slug line]*
-------------------------------------------------- *[page break]* --------------------------------------------------

CONTINUED
                      CHARACTER (CONT'D)
            . . . continued on the top of the next page.

                              FADE OUT

NEVER SAY DIE      *[series title]*

"If It Quacks Like a Duck ..."    *[episode title]*

#40345-085      *[episode number]*

<u>ACT ONE</u>      *[denotes the act]*

A      *[denotes the scene]*

*[The script actually begins about 1/3 to 1/2 way down the page, as indicated below. Some sitcoms start with a TEASER, a short scene that may or may not be connected to the main story line. Others start with a COLD OPENING.]*

*[ In a sitcom script, EACH SCENE BEGINS ON A NEW PAGE.]*

*[Note that slug lines are CAPITALIZED AND UNDERLINED. All characters who appear in the scene are listed just below the slug line. The description of the action is in ALL CAPS, and the names of the characters are UNDERLINED.]*

FADE IN:
*[double space]*
<u>INT. BUS STATION - DAY</u>
(Alex, Ginger, Ticker Taker)
*[double space]*
<u>ALEX</u> AND <u>GINGER</u> HURRY THROUGH THE DOOR AND RUSH TOWARD THE TICKET
BOOTH.  BOTH ARE LOADED DOWN WITH SUITCASES AND BAGS OF CHRISTMAS
PRESENTS.
*[double space]*
                  ALEX

    (GASPING FOR BREATH) I never thought

    we'd make it!

*[Note that in sitcom scripts, the dialogue is DOUBLE-SPACED and the parentheticals are IN ALL CAPS.)*

FADE IN ON EXTERIOR OF SUBURBAN MIDDLE-
CLASS HOUSE.  DAYTIME.  LAWN IS WELL
MANICURED.  CAMERA TRUCKS PAST SIDE OF
HOUSE TO BACK YARD.  THERE IS A SAND BOX
AND TRICYCLE.  MAIN CHARACTER, BOB
ANDERSON, IS STANDING AT THE BARBECUE,
PREPARING HAMBURGERS.

<u>MUSIC:  UPBEAT POP ROCK, UP FULL, THEN
UNDER AS BILL MOYERS STARTS NARRATION.</u>

<u>MOYERS  (OFF-CAMERA, VOICE-OVER)</u>:  Bob
Anderson, age thirty-two, self-employed
heating and air-conditioner installer
and repairman.  He considers himself
fairly well off.  Moderately successful.
Happily married, with two bright
youngsters.  Not too many debts.  He
doesn't realize, however, how close he
is to having his world crumble beneath
his feet.

MOYERS WALKS INTO THE FRAME.

<u>MUSIC FADES OUT.</u>

<u>MOYERS</u>:  How's it going, Bob?

<u>ANDERSON (GLANCING UP)</u>:  Oh, hi there.
You're just in time for some burgers.

<u>MOYERS</u>:  Thanks, maybe I will.  You
know, we were talking the other day
about last week's election . . .

<u>ANDERSON (TRYING TO REMAIN CHEERFUL)</u>:
Yeh, and you were getting on me for not
voting.  Well, like I said, I really
couldn't tell any difference between the

26

| VIDEO | AUDIO |
|---|---|
| FADE IN ON EXTERIOR OF SUBURBAN MIDDLE-CLASS HOUSE. DAYTIME.  LAWN IS WELL MANI-CURED.  CAMERA TRUCKS PAST SIDE OF HOUSE TO BACK YARD. THERE IS A SAND BOX AND TRICYCLE.  MAIN CHARACTER, BOB ANDERSON, IS STANDING AT THE BARBECUE, PREPARING HAMBURGERS. | MUSIC:  UPBEAT POP ROCK, UP FULL, THEN UNDER AS BILL MOYERS STARTS NARRATION.<br><br>MOYERS  (OFF-CAMERA, VOICE-OVER:<br>Bob Anderson, age thirty-two, self-employed heating and air conditioner installer and repairman.  He considers himself fairly well off.  Moderately successful.  Happily married, with two bright youngsters.  Not too many debts.  He doesn't realize, however, how close he is to having his world crumble beneath his feet. |
| MOYERS WALKS INTO THE FRAME.  ANDERSON GLANCES UP, NODS HIS HEAD AND CONTINUES TO TEND HIS GRILL. | MUSIC FADES OUT<br>MOYERS:  How's it going, Bob?<br>ANDERSON:  Oh, hi there.  You're just in time for some burgers.<br>MOYERS:  Thanks, maybe I will.  You know, we were talking the other day about last week's election . . . |
| ANDERSON GLANCES AT MOYERS, TRYING TO REMAIN CHEERFUL, BUT IS SLIGHTLY DEFENSIVE. | ANDERSON:  Yeh, and you were getting on me for not voting.  Well, like I said, I really couldn't tell any difference between the candidates. |

27

FADE IN:

EXT.     SUBURBAN MIDDLE-CLASS HOUSE     DAY

The lawn is well manicured in a pleasant middle-class
neighborhood.  The CAMERA TRUCKS past the side of the house
to the back yard.  Maintain WIDE SHOT of patio area with
sand box and tricycle.  BOB ANDERSON is standing at the
barbecue preparing hamburgers.  CAMERA SLOWLY DOLLIES IN to
WAIST SHOT of Anderson.  MUSIC is soft pop rock, up full,
then under NARRATION.

> BILL MOYERS
> (off-camera, voice-over)
> Bob Anderson, age thirty-two,
> self-employed heating and air
> conditioner installer and
> repairman.  He considers
> himself fairly well off.
> Moderately successful.
> Happily married, with two
> bright youngsters.  Not too
> many debts.  He doesn't
> realize, however, how close
> he is to having his world
> crumble beneath his feet.

EXT.     ANDERSON'S BACK YARD.          SAME

TWO-SHOT of Moyers and Anderson as Moyers walks around
the corner of the house.  CAMERA PANS and TIGHTENS shot
as Moyers joins Anderson at the grill.  MUSIC out.

> MOYERS
> How's it going, Bob?

Anderson glances up at Moyers, nods amicably in
recognition and continues to tend the grill.

> ANDERSON
> Oh, hi there.  You're just in
> time for some burgers.

> MOYERS
> Thanks, maybe I will.
> (after a slight pause)
> You know, we were talking the
> other day about last week's
> election . . .

ANGLE FAVORING ANDERSON

> ANDERSON
> (trying to remain cheerful)

| Action | Sound |
|---|---|
| <u>FADE IN</u> on: | <u>Music</u>: |
| 1a. EXTERIOR of middle-class house. Daytime. Lawn is well manicured. CAMERA TRUCKS past the side of the house into the back yard. | Upbeat pop rock music, up full, then under narration. |
| 1b. WIDE SHOT includes sand box and tricycle. We see BOB ANDERSON standing at the barbecue preparing hamburgers. | <u>Bill Moyers</u>: |
| 1c. DOLLY IN to WAIST SHOT of Anderson. | (off-camera, voice-over) Bob Anderson, age thirty-two, self-employed heating and air conditioner installer and repairman. He considers himself fairly well off. Moderately successful. Happily married, with two bright youngsters. Not too many debts. He doesn't realize, however, how close he is to having his world crumble beneath his feet. |
| 2a. TWO-SHOT of Moyers and Anderson as Moyers walks around the corner of the house. CAMERA PANS and TIGHTENS shot as Moyers joins Anderson at the grill. | <u>Music</u>: <br><br> Fades out. <br><br> <u>Moyers</u>: <br><br> (on camera) How's it going, Bob? |
| 2b. Anderson glances up at Moyers, nods amicably and continues to tend the grill. | <u>Anderson</u>: <br><br> Oh, hi there. You're just in time for some burgers. <br><br> <u>Moyers</u>: <br><br> Thanks, maybe I will. You know, we were talking the other day about last week's election . . . |
| 3a. OVER-THE-SHOULDER shot of Anderson. Anderson tries to remain cheerful. | <u>Anderson</u>: <br><br> Yeh, and you were getting on me for not voting. Well, like I said |

<u>SFX: HORSE AND CARRIAGE: FADE IN, UP FULL 5 SECS AND FADE UNDER</u>

<u>ANNOUNCER</u>:             It's three A.M. in the French Quarter of New

Orleans.  How'd you like the best cup of

coffee in town?  And a beignet [ben-<u>yay</u>]?

That's a square donut without a hole.

<u>SFX: SEGUE TO RESTAURANT AMBIENCE, UP FULL 5 SECS AND FADE UNDER</u>

<u>ANNOUNCER</u>:             This is the place.  Morning call.  Find a

stool at one of the elbow-worn marble

counters, and while you're waiting for your

order, take a look around.

<u>MUSIC:   SEGUE TO ZYDECO BAND, UP FULL 5 SECS AND FADE UNDER</u>

<u>ANNOUNCER</u>:             The place hasn't changed much in the past

hundred years.  Same counters, same foot

rail.  Same mirrors where you can watch and

be watched, sipping coffee and sprinkling

powdered sugar on hot beignets [ben-<u>yays</u>].

Only in New Orleans . . . Just one of the

places that make Delta Airlines what it is

. . . The wings of enchantment.

<u>SFX: AUDIENCE APPLAUDS, UP FULL 5 SECS AND CROSS FADE TO</u>
       <u>MUSIC THEME</u>

<u>ANNOUNCER</u>:          Ask about our special fares to New Orleans
                    and points south.  At Delta, we love to fly
                    . . . And it shows!

<u>MUSIC:   FINAL THEME, UP FULL 5 SECS AND FADE OUT</u>

THE GIRL IN THE GRASS

FADE IN:

EXT. ANGLE ON BIRD FEEDER -- DAY

A mild winter morning in suburban Atlanta, Georgia.  In CLOSE,
finches, chickadees, sparrows flutter around a large window
feeder, gobbling up the scarce seed.

The SOUNDS we hear, however, are <u>not</u> those of birds.  Gradually
we are aware of the RUSTLE OF BEDDING and SOFT HUMAN VOICES.

We are looking through the glass of a large upstairs bedroom
window.

>                    MAN'S VOICE
>               (suggestive nuzzling)
>      Mmmmmmmm?

>                    WOMAN'S VOICE
>               (drowsy; trying not to
>               wake up)
>      Nuh-uh . . .

>                    MAN'S VOICE
>      Mmmmm . . . mmmmm?

The birds peck aggressively at the feeder, competing with one
another for winter food.

>                    MAN'S VOICE
>               (trying to be sexy)
>      Come on . . . turn over . . . come on.

>                    WOMAN'S VOICE
>               (trying desperately not
>               to wake up)
>      Matt, please . . . let me sleep just a
>      few more minutes . . .
>                    (beat)
>      Tonight . . . I promise . . . tonight
>      . . .

Her voice trails off.  A CLOCK RADIO snaps on.  A bright MOZART
CONCERTO plays.

>                    MAN'S VOICE
>      Damn.

ANGLE - CLOCK RADIO

It is 6:00 a.m.  A man's hand smacks the snooze alarm.  The music
stops.

### If I Had Wings

## Act One

Sixteen-year-old gymnast STACY WELDON [Protagonist]* just
misses executing a difficult routine on the parallel bars in a
Houston gym.  She expresses frustration to her SPOTTER, and
determines to get it right.  [Foreshadowing]  Her COACH emerges
from the office and hurries over to them with the news that a
spot has opened on the U.S. gymnastic team in the Olympic trials.
She leaves for Denver on Saturday.  [Inciting incident]  Stacy is
ecstatic that her dreams are coming true.  Later in her small
apartment she calls her mom and dad in Florida.  We learn of the
sacrifices that have been made, that Stacy has been away from
home for almost eight months--but now "it's all paying off."
Next day in the gym, Stacy tries the same difficult routine one
more time.  She loses her grip and falls hard to the floor on her
right forearm.  She's in pain, and can't move her fingers.  [Act
One turning point]

## Act Two

At the hospital Stacy learns the awful truth: her right
forearm is broken in two places.  She will miss the Olympic
trials and will in all probability never have another chance to
make the Olympic games.  She is heart-broken.  All her hard work,
all the sacrifices--for nothing!  Her parents come and take her
back to Boca Raton.  Stacy's arm starts to heal, but not her
spirits.  She is depressed.  She has to undergo physical therapy
and while there she meets a 10-year-old Cuban boy named ROCKY
CONTRERAS.  [Midpoint scene]  Rocky is in therapy "because he
keeps breaking his bones."  Actually, he has terminal bone
cancer, but is nonetheless upbeat and cheerful.  When he finds
out Stacy was a gymnast, he tells her about some local kids with
disabilities who are putting together their own little Olympics

and are looking for a coach. Stacy isn't interested. She's still feeling sorry for herself. Rocky persists, however, and finally she gives in. She meets the group--all kids like Rocky who are suffering from terminal diseases, and who, like Rocky, have positive attitudes. As Stacy begins to work with them, she finds her own attitude starting to change. They work toward their "little Olympics" and Stacy is looking forward to it. Then she gets a call from her coach in Houston; they want to bring her to Denver to work with the Olympic team as a coach. Stacy will get to the Olympics after all! She excitedly agrees. *[Act Two turning point]*

Act Three

She tells the kids at the physical therapy center about this new opportunity. She feels guilty, she's afraid how they might respond--but they are all excited for her. Stacy packs and gets ready to leave. She then gets a call from Rocky; the kids have a going away present for her. Stacy stops off at the center on her way to the airport. The kids put on a "performance" for her, showing her the things she has taught them. Stacy's touched. In that moment she realizes that these kids now mean more to her than going to the Olympics, and she cancels her trip. *[Climax]* Later, the disabled kids perform for an appreciative public audience, and at the end Rocky presents Stacy with a bouquet of flowers. She tearfully accepts them, and waves to the applauding crowd of parents, doctors, nurses and physical therapists. In a way, Stacy makes it to the Olympics after all. *[Denouement]*

_ _ _ _ _ _ _ _ _ _

* Note that in this story, there is no outside *Antagonist*. The conflict is essentially an internal one within Stacy as she struggles to overcome her great disappointment and to find a new direction for her life.

# BIBLIOGRAPHY

## General Research and Writing

Barzun, Jacques, and Henry F. Graff. *The Modern Researcher*. 5th ed. Fort Worth: Harcourt Brace Jovanovich College Publishers, 1992.

Hopper, Vincent F., and Cedric Gale. *Essentials of Writing*. 4th ed., revised by Benjamin W. Griffith, Jr. Hauppauge, NY: Barron's Educational Series, Inc., 1991.

Maimon, Elaine P., Barbara F. Nodine, and Finbarr W. O'Connor. *Thinking, Reasoning, and Writing*. New York: Longman, 1989.

Provost, Gary. *100 Ways to Improve Your Writing*. New York: Penguin Group/Mentor Book, 1985.

Wood, Donald N. *Designing the Effective Message: Critical Thinking and Communication*. 2nd ed. Dubuque, IA: Kendall/Hunt Publishing Company, 1996.

## Scriptwriting Guides

Armer, Alan. *Writing the Screenplay: TV and Film*. 2nd ed. Belmont, CA: Wadsworth, 1993.

Dancyger, Ken, and Jeff Rush. *Alternative Scriptwriting: Writing Beyond the Rules*. Boston: Focal Press, 1991.

Dimaggio, Madeline. *How to Write for Television*. New York: Prentice-Hall, 1990.

Lee, Robert, and Robert Misiorowski. *Script Models: A Handbook for the Media Writer*. New York: Hastings House, Publishers, 1978.

Matrazzo, Donna. *Corporate Scriptwriting Book*. Portland, OR: Communicom Publishing Company, 1985.

Meeske, Milan D., and R. C. Norris. *Copywriting for the Electronic Media*. 2nd ed. Belmont, CA: Wadsworth, 1992.

Seger, Linda. *The Art of Adaptation: Turning Fact and Fiction into Film*. New York: Henry Holt and Company, 1992.

_____. *Creating Unforgettable Characters*. New York: Henry Holt and Company, 1990.

_____. *Making a Good Script Great*. 2nd ed. Hollywood: Samuel French, 1994.

Vogler, Christopher. *The Writer's Journey: Mythic Structure for Storytellers and Screenwriters*. Studio City, CA: Michael Wiese Productions, 1992.

Vorhaus, John. *The Comic Toolbox: How To Be Funny Even If You're Not*. Los Angeles: Silman-James Press, 1994.

## Style and Format Manuals

Associated Press. *The Associated Press Stylebook and Libel Manual*. Rev. ed. Reading, MA: Addison-Wesley Publishing Company, 1987.

Gibaldi, Joseph. *MLA Handbook for Writers of Research Papers*. 4th ed. New York: The Modern Language Association of America, 1995.

*Publication Manual of the American Psychological Association*. 4th ed. Washington DC: American Psychological Association, 1994.

Turabian, Kate L. *A Manual for Writers of Term Papers, Theses, and Dissertations*. 6th ed. Revised by John Grossman and Alice Bennett. Chicago: University of Chicago Press, 1996.

University of Chicago Press. *The Chicago Manual of Style for Authors, Editors, and Copywriters*. 13th ed. Chicago: University of Chicago Press, 1982.

## Electronic Citations

Crouse, Maurice. <crousem@cc.memphis.edu>. "Citing Electronic Information In History Papers." Rev. ed. <http://www.people.memphis.edu/~mcrouse/elcite.html>. 10 February 1996.

Guernsey, Lisa. "Cyberspace Citations." *Chronicle of Higher Education,* 12 January 1996: pp. A18, 20.

Harnack, Andrew, and Eugene Kleppinger. "Citing the Sites: MLA-Style Guidelines and Models for Documenting Internet Sources," version 1.3. In *Beyond the MLA Handbook: Documenting Electronic Sources on the Internet.* 10 June 1996. Available [Online]: <http://english.ttu.edu/kairos/1.2/inbox/mla_archive.html> [6 May 1999].

Li, Xia, and Nancy Crane. *The Official Internet World Guide to Electronic Styles: A Handbook to Citing Electronic Information.* Westport, CT: Meckler, 1996.

Tent, Jan. "Citation Guides for Electronic Documents." International Federation of Library Associations and Institution: [IFLA]. 15 March 1996.

## Writing and Language Guides

Campbell, William Giles, Stephen Vaughn Ballou, and Carol Slade. *Form and Style: Theses, Reports, Term Papers.* 7th ed. Boston: Houghton Mifflin Company, 1986.

Cooper, Charles W., and Edmund J. Robins. *The Term Paper: A Manual and Model.* 4th ed. Stanford, CA: Stanford University Press, 1967.

Flesch, Rudolf, and A. H. Lass. *A New Guide to Better Writing.* New York: Warner Books, 1977.

Harnack, Andrew. *Writing Research Papers: A Student Guide for Use with Opposing Viewpoints.* San Diego: Greenhaven Press, 1994.

*The Merriam-Webster Concise Handbook for Writers.* Springfield, MA: Merriam-Webster, Incorporated, 1991.

*Merriam-Webster's Guide to Punctuation and Style.* Springfield, MA: Merriam-Webster, Incorporated, 1995.

*REA's Handbook of English Grammar, Style, and Writing.* Piscataway, NJ: Research and Education Association, 1995.

Roth, Audrey J. *The Research Paper: Process, Form, & Content.* 6th ed. Belmont, CA: Wadsworth Publishing Company, 1989.

Rubin, Rebecca B., Alan M. Rubin, and Linda J. Piele. *Communication Research: Strategies and Sources.* Belmont, CA: Wadsworth Publishing Company, 1986.

Strunk, William, Jr., and E. B. White. *The Elements of Style.* 3rd ed. New York: Macmillan Publishing, 1979.

Turabian, Kate L. *Student's Guide for Writing College Papers.* 3rd ed. Chicago: University of Chicago Press, 1976.

Walker, Melissa. *Writing Research Papers: A Norton Guide.* New York: W. W. Norton & Company, 1984.

Winkler, Anthony C. *Writing the Research Paper: A Handbook with both the MLA and APA Documentation Styles.* Fort Worth: Harcourt Brace College Publishers, 1994.

## Reference Works

Andrews, Robert. *The Columbia Dictionary of Quotations.* New York: Columbia University Press, 1993.

Bartlett, John, and Justin Kaplan. *Familiar Quotations: A Collection of Passages, Phrases and Proverbs Traced to Their Sources in Ancient and Modern Literature.* 16th ed. Boston: Little, Brown and Company, 1992.

Kipfer, Barbara Ann. *Roget's 21st Century Thesaurus in Dictionary Form: The Essential Reference for Home, School, or Office.* New York: Dell Publishing, 1992.

Laird, Charlton Grant, and William Lutz. *Webster's New World Thesaurus.* Rev. ed. New York: Simon and Schuster, 1985.

Miner, Margaret. *The New International Dictionary of Quotations.* 2nd ed. New York: Dutton, 1993.

*The Oxford Dictionary of Quotations.* 3rd ed. New York: Oxford University Press, 1986.

Roget, Peter Mark, and Robert L. Chapman. *Roget's International Thesaurus.* 4th ed. New York: Harper & Row, 1977.

*Roget's II: The New Thesaurus.* Boston: Houghton Mifflin, 1988.